Sources of Religious
Sentiment

Sources of
Religious
Sentiment

BY MAURICE HALBWACHS

Translated by John A. Spaulding

THE FREE PRESS OF GLENCOE, INC.

A DIVISION OF THE CROWELL-COLLIER PUBLISHING COMPANY

PREFACE

URKHEIM, THE FOUNDER OF THE FRENCH school of sociology, has presented in various studies an original and profound theory of religion. The work here offered to the reader is as exact, even literal, a summary of these ideas as possible—ideas that were given final form in his last work, published in 1912, *The Elementary Forms of the Religious Life. The Australian System of Totemism.*[1]

1. All quotations not credited to a particular author or work are taken from this work.

Preface

We do not claim to give in this limited space a brief sketch of the wealth and range of such a work. We cannot suggest in detail the discussions occasioned by this thesis both among ethnologists, upon the best works of whom it draws, and among historians of religion and philosophers. But the writers felt that, even reduced to its lowest terms, it deserved henceforth to be known and considered by a wider public.

We have almost always employed the author's own words. This will make it unnecessary to repeat at the beginning of each page: "Durkheim states . . ."; and we will offer no apology for the number of quotations.

In the Bibliography will be found the list of books, monographs and articles mentioned in the text.

CONTENTS

Contents

Sources of Religious Sentiment

HOW MAY RELIGION
BE DEFINED?

THE EXPLANATION OF RELIGIOUS BELIEF given by eighteenth-century philosophers today seems rather superficial to us. Starting with the principle *is fecit cui prodest* (the author is the one advantaged), they declared that the caste of priests, astute personages greedy for money and authority, had invented it from beginning to end; the rascally priests would then, supposedly, have exploited the credulity of those who had faith. Let us not be unduly severe as to Voltaire, Diderot, the Encyclopedists, and their like. Historical science in their day was still unknown. They did their best to lift the veil. It was no small achievement merely to have made the gesture. It is nonetheless true that they were wrong to see in religions only arbitrary and artificial constructions.

The point of view of modern sociologists is quite different. They do not believe that a human institution that is based solely on error and falsehood can have lasted for so long and possess such vitality to this very day. Religions must surely be based on natural foundations; otherwise, "they would have encountered a resistance in the very nature of things that they could not have overcome." To be sure, "when one considers only the literal formulas, these religious beliefs and observances at times seem to be disconcerting and one may feel tempted to attribute them to a sort of basic error of judgment. But underneath the symbolism one must know how to reach the reality that it represents and that gives it its true meaning." Since a religion corresponds to certain permanent needs of mankind (and it must do this, since, in spite of its apparent contradiction of reality, it is preserved), we have no right to say that it is wholly false. Taken in this sense, every religion contains an element of truth, however crude and bar-

barous or however strange and complicated it may appear to us. This element of truth is what interests us. We must try to discover what useful functions religions fulfill in society.

To be sure, many differences exist among religions, due to the fact that they have developed in societies more or less complex, as the case may be. But each of them is well adapted to that type of society in which it functions: if one really understood the nature of one of them, however simple, one might perhaps at the same time reach the essential nature of all religion. Besides, there are reasons for studying the simplest religions first. Primarily, "we can only succeed in understanding the most recent religions by tracing historically the way in which they have developed, stage by stage." So we must begin at the beginning, or go back to the most primitive form, the simplest form of all religion with which we are acquainted. To be sure, again, we shall not be able to prove that this simplest religion is also the original form of all the rest. But as a convenient hypothesis and guiding idea so much may be granted: we surely need a leading clue to conduct us through the maze of religious facts that are often so obscure and composed of so many elements. On the other hand, just because the institutions of inferior societies are simpler, they are easier to study. In them individuals play lesser roles than in our modern societies. Besides, these groups are restricted and change slowly. They exemplify "an intellectual and moral uniformity only rare examples of which are found in more advanced societies. Everything belongs to all in common. Movements are stereotyped; under similar circumstances everyone performs the same movements, and this conformity of conduct merely translates the conformity of thought. . . . At the same time that everything is uniform, everything is also simple. There is nothing so simple as these myths made of a single theme repeated an infinite number of times, nor as these rites composed of a small number of gestures repeated to the point of weariness. Popular or priestly imagination has as yet had neither the time nor the means of refining upon them. . . . No accessory, nothing secondary, no luxurious developments have supervened to conceal the basic theme. All in it is reduced to the indispensable, to the very basic necessities of religion." Thus we are sure of reaching in them the essential features of religion, in their clearest form.

But a preliminary question arises. Are there really in these primitive societies beliefs that deserve to be called religious? And what are we to understand by the term "religion"? Undoubtedly, we have to start here with a provisional definition. What we intend is simply to "point out a certain number of external signs, easily perceptible, that make it possible to recognize religious phenomena wherever they occur and to avoid their confusion with others." With this in mind, we shall try not to restrict ourselves to our ideas of religion hitherto formed—ideas explicable by our education, which we have received from our environment. We will compare all religions, ancient and modern, with which we are able to become acquainted, simple and refined alike, for we have no right to exclude some any more than the others. And we shall be especially suspicious of the current definitions, almost all of which are too restricted.

Must we say with Spencer and Max Müller that every religion puts us in relation with a world of the supernatural? Is religion above all an attempt to reach and express what is beyond us? "Certainly the feeling of mystery has played an important role in certain of them, especially in Christianity." But, first of all, it has not always been so, not in all the diverse periods of the history of Christianity. Above all, the feeling of the supernatural "appears only very late in the history of religions: it is completely foreign not merely to what are called primitive peoples but also to all that have not yet achieved a certain stage of intellectual culture." This remark may seem astonishing. The conceptions of savages and of the men of antiquity seem so strange to us that we are unable to believe that they did not seem so to them as well. But this is incorrect. The savage thinks it entirely natural "that one should be able to command the elements with voice or gesture, stop or precipitate the courses of the stars, bring rain or cause it to cease, etc. The rites employed for the fertility of the soil or the fecundity of the animal species with which they are fed" are in his eyes as rational as the measures of farmers and agriculturists. The forces that he thus sets in play are as familiar to him as gravity and electricity to the present-day physicist. Besides, in order to rise to the idea of the supernatural, one must first know what is the natural order. Such distinctions are entirely modern: they are a conquest of positive science. Savages know nothing of what we call the necessity of the natural order. That is why "the miraculous interventions attributed by the ancients to their gods were not miracles in their eyes" in the modern sense of the word. They marveled at them *(miracula, mirabilia)* but saw nothing mysterious about them. Can we say that if men imagined religious beings and forces, it was to explain whatever appeared unexpected, exceptional, or abnormal to them? On the contrary, generally, "the gods serve much less to explain monstrosities, curiosities, and anomalies than the customary processes of the universe, the astral movements, the seasonal rhythm, the annual vegetative growth, the persistence of species, etc." Far from having been "restricted to the negative roles of intervention," starting with the simplest religions known to us, the sacred beings have "had the essential function of sustaining the normal course of life in a positive manner." Thus the idea of mystery assumes the center of the stage in a small number of advanced religions: it does not suffice to define religion in general.

It has been said that every religious cult is addressed to a god or gods. Between the idea of divinity and that of religion there is supposed to be so intimate a relation that it might even be defined as the belief in gods. True, the spirits of the dead and spirits of every sort and rank are also the objects of rites. As the minimal definition of religion, we will therefore suppose the belief in spiritual beings or in conscious and more or less personalized causes, gifted with superior powers. As such causes may be affected only by means of invocations, prayers, offerings or sacrifices, we shall be led, like Frazer, to distinguish clearly from religions all those superstitious practices observed among savages who know no such rites and who do not believe in such beings. All such practices would then be relegated to magic and would have nothing of the religious character.

Nevertheless, even outside of primitive societies, there exist large and undoubtedly religious communities that also do not know the meaning of gods or spirits. Godless religions exist—for example, Buddhism. The Buddhist seeks only to escape from this world in perpetual flux and devoted to sorrow, and counts on nothing but his own efforts to achieve this work of salvation. He prays to no gods but retires within himself and meditates. At first Buddha was considered merely as "the wisest of men." He is a saint whose cult is one solely of commemoration, for, having entered into Nirvana, "he can no longer affect the course of human events." So it is with Jainism, and with Brahminism, both of which are religions diverted from their original course. In Brahminism the figures of the ancient gods have become effaced: Brahma is enthroned far too high above the world of humanity for anything to be perceptible but an impersonal, abstract principle. Moreover, even in deistic religions there exist many rites "completely independent of any idea of gods or spiritual beings." Such are many proscriptions: "the Bible commands woman to live in isolation for a definite period of every month; it requires a similar isolation during the period of confinement; it forbids the yoking together of horse and ass, the wearing of a garment in which hemp is combined with linen." But none of all these commandments are any concern of Jehovah's, and none is explicable by the belief in Him. The sacrifice of the Vedas "is omnipotent in itself, without any divine influence." Far more important, it is to sacrifice that the origin not only of men but of the gods themselves is attributed. Thus there are godless rites and even rites that are the source of the gods themselves: nor are they any the less religious. Religion cannot, then, be defined by the idea of gods or spirits.

If at this point we look for a character common no longer to some religions but to every religious faith, even those existing merely as the debris of religions that have disappeared, which constitute the subject matter of folklore—May-tree festivals, carnivals, and the popular beliefs still existing among our peasant populations with reference to evil spirits or local demons—the result will be as follows: "All known religious faiths . . . presuppose a classification of things whether real or ideal as conceived by men into two opposed classes and genera, usually indicated by two distinct terms that may be adequately translated by the words *profane* and *sacred*. . . . We must not understand by sacred things merely such personal beings as are called gods or spirits; a rock, a tree, a spring of water, a pebble, a piece of wood, a house, or, in a word, anything whatever may be sacred. A rite itself may have this character. . . . Words, terms, and formulas exist that are not to be pronounced save by the mouths of consecrated persons who themselves are sacred." But how are sacred things distinguished from the profane? Are they superior to the latter, especially to man, in dignity and power? But "it is not enough for something to be subordinated to something else to secure that the second is sacred with reference to the former. Slaves are dependent on their master, subjects on their chief, inferior classes on the governing classes." Now it is only metaphorically possible to say that the king, master, chief, or the upper classes are sacred in the eyes of their slaves, their subjects," and so on. On the contrary, man does not always feel himself in a dependent state with regard to sacred beings or to the gods themselves. "The fetish with which one is displeased is beaten. . . . In order to procure rain, stones are cast into the spring or the sacred lake in which the god of rain is supposed to live." Besides, the gods need man as much as man the gods. "They would die without offerings and sacrifices." Actually, the sacred is not superior to the profane: what explains the distinction between them is a difference not in rank but in quality. They are of different sorts. True, many things are different in certain respects without so clear a line of demarcation among them. But the difference here is peculiar in being absolute. "There is no other example in the history of human thought of two categories of things so deeply different and so radically opposed. . . . The traditional opposition between good and evil is nothing compared with this, for good and evil are two contrary species of a single genus, namely, the moral genus . . . whereas the sacred and profane are like separate genera." In order to pass from one to the other of these worlds, one must die and be reborn. Ceremonies of initiation are considered to realize such death and rebirth, not symbolically but literally. This explains the proscriptions that prevent confusion or contact between the two sorts of objects and at all events compel the use of special precautions when it is necessary to bring them into contact with one another. "Sacred things are those protected and isolated by such proscriptions; profane things, those to which they apply and which must remain at a distance from the former." Religion may thus be defined as an interdependent whole composed of beliefs and rites related to sacred things.

This definition however is incomplete. Indeed, magic also consists of beliefs and rites. It possesses its own myths, dogmas, ceremonies, sacrifices, and prayers. Not infrequently the sacred beings themselves, such especially as the souls of the dead, or demons, are simultaneously the object of religious rites and magic practices. "There are even certain regular, official divinities that are invoked by the magician. Sometimes they are the gods of a foreign people: for instance, the Greek magicians appealed to the gods of the Assyrians, Egyptians, or Hebrews. Sometimes they are even national divinities: Hecate and Diana were the objects of a magic cult; the Virgin, Christ, the saints have been similarly employed by Christian magicians." And yet magic is not to be confused with religion. What proves this is "the marked repugnance of religion for magic and, on the other hand, the hostility of the latter to the former." The magician applies himself to the profanation of things sacred. "In the Black Mass, for instance, the consecrated wafer is profaned. One's back is turned to the altar and the service begins at the left instead of at the right hand." As Messrs. Hubert and Mauss have demonstrated, "in magical procedures there is something basically antireligious."

How is magic to be distinguished from religion? Observe that "no religion without a church is to be found in history. At times the church is narrowly national, at times it extends beyond frontiers; at times it includes an entire people (as in the case of Rome, Athens, or the Hebrew people), at times only a fraction of them (the various Christian societies since the appearance of Protestantism); at times the church is governed by a priestly body," at other times it has no chief. But wherever we find a religious life, it extends to the whole of a definite group. So it is even with private cults, family or corporation cults, all of which moreover merely represent special forms of a more general religion, like so many chapels of a vaster cathedral. Magical beliefs, on the contrary, though spread throughout extensive strata of population, "no longer bind and unite their adherents into a single group. . . . There is no magic Church. . . . The magician possesses a clientele, not a church, and his clients may very well be ignorant of one another." If sometimes magicians combine—if, for example, there are societies of sorcerers—the magician in general is rather an isolated figure: far from seeking company, he avoids it. But, above all, in such assemblies only magicians participate, not those for whose benefit they operate. On the contrary, a church includes not only priests but also embraces in its bosom all the faithful. There is, therefore, in magic, no church.

Thus a definition of religion exists: ". . . an interdependent system of faiths and practices relating to things sacred—that is, to such things as are separate and proscribed, faiths and practices uniting all their adherents in a single community, known as a Church."

ARE THERE RUDIMENTARY RELIGIONS?

Animism and Naturalism

ARE THERE, AMONG ALL THE KNOWN RELIgions, some that may be called rudimentary in the sense of presupposing no other and simpler ones from which they might be derived? The problem is not new. It was faced at a very early period. And its solution has been sought in two different directions. It has indeed been noted that in almost all religious systems, old or recent, two religions may be distinguished—associated and at times blended with one another yet very different. "One appeals to the things of nature, either the great cosmic forces like the winds, the rivers, the stars, the sky, etc., or the manifold objects occupying the earth's surface—plants, animals, rocks, etc.; and for this reason it has been called *naturalism*. The other's object is the spiritual beings, spirits, souls, genies, demons, divinities properly so called, animated and conscious agents like man himself" but that, in particular, are invisible and not sensuously perceptible to him. "This religion of spirits is called *animism*." Now, in order to explain the coexistence of these two kinds of cults, two different theories have been sustained: in the eyes of some, animism is the primitive religion and the religion of nature is derived from it; in the opinion of others, the cult of nature manifested itself first and produced the cult of spirits. Let us examine the value of these two explanations.

In the animistic theory it is first demonstrated how the idea of the soul originated among men who as yet possessed no religious faith. This is the point of view of Tylor and Spencer. They start from an illusion of which primitive men are supposed to have been the victims, caused by their dreams. The savage confounds dream and reality. "Therefore, when he dreams that he has visited a distant country, he believes that he has really gone there. But he can have gone there only if two beings exist within him: one, his body, which has been left lying on the ground and which he rediscovers in the same position on awakening; the other, which has moved through space during the same period of time as he has slumbered." When he dreams of conversing with one of his companions who is detained at a distance, he similarly supposes that the other is composed of two beings, one of which has been left lying wherever he was sleeping while the other came to meet him. From this arises the idea of a double, of another self that under certain circumstances can free itself and depart from us temporarily. This double bears our own image. But it has greater mobility than our body, "since it can traverse vast distances in an instant of time. It is both more malleable and more plastic; for in order to leave the body it must pass through the orifices of the organism, especially the nose and mouth. It is therefore conceived of as composed of matter, to be sure, but of a much subtler and more ethereal substance than any which we know. . . . This double is the soul." Indeed, for many primitive people the soul is merely an image of the body. And it seems quite natural to confuse this double with the soul, since one supposedly withdraws during sleep, and, similarly, during sleep life and thought seem interrupted.

But for the soul to become the object of a cult it must be transformed into spirit. This occurs when man dies. Death resembles sleep in that the soul is separated from the body. But this time the separation is final. "Here, then, are detached spirits without organisms, set free to wander through space. . . . These human souls have human needs and passions; therefore they seek to mingle with the lives of their companions of yesterday, to aid or injure them according to the feelings they retain toward them." Moreover, whether they enter bodies to produce all sorts of disorder there or to fortify them, they can do much good or evil. To them are attributed sicknesses as well as the states of inspiration that raise a man above his normal self. Then "the attempt is made either to conciliate their good will or to appease them when irritated: thence the offerings, sacrifices, prayers, in short all the apparatus of religious observances." Since it is death that transforms the soul from a mere vital principle to a spirit, almost to a divinity, "the first cult known to humanity is that of the dead, of the souls of ancestors. Thus the first rites are supposed to have been the mortuary ones; the first sacrifices, to have been sacrifices of food intended to satisfy the needs of the dead; the first altars, to have been tombs."

There is no explanation here of how other spirits came to be imagined and assigned to the direction of the various phenomena of nature, of how "a cult of nature was established beside the ancestor cult." Accounts of this have been given in two different manners. According to Tylor, primitive man, like a child, is inclined to confuse the animate with the inanimate. As soon as man is believed to be a body endowed with a spirit, primitive man admits that things have spirits too. Hence arises the idea of cosmic spirits residing in things and producing everything that happens in or concerning them—the flow of watercourses, the movement of the stars, vegetation, etc. Since man depends on these things themselves, he depends on these spirits. Thus he renders them a cult. Spencer, on the contrary, thinks that, like the higher animals, primitive man can distinguish animate beings from inanimate things. According to him, a different sort of confusion explains the passage from the cult of spirits to that of nature. In many primitive tribes individuals were given the names of certain natural objects, animals, plants, stars, etc. Later it was forgotten that these names were merely metaphors, and the ancestors were thought of as having really been animals, plants, and stars. This accounts for the tendering of the same cult to these objects as to the ancestors themselves. Thus the religion of nature came into existence—an explanation of little value, since "all the personal recollections left by an ancestor in the memory of man" make such a confusion difficult. How, without additional reason beside these names, should primitive men themselves have admitted that men could have been born of mountains, stars, animals, or plants? Let us therefore abide by Tylor's theory, "the authority of which is still very considerable," and examine its different elements.

Are we supposed to believe that dreams gave men the idea that in each of them exists a double that can leave the body and return to it? But was no other, simpler explanation for dream illusions possible? "Why, for instance, should the sleeper not have supposed that during his sleep he was capable of seeing to a great distance? Less effort of the imagination would be required to attribute such a power to one's self than to construct the very complex notion of a double, made of an ethereal substance and semi-invisible, of which direct experience offers no example." Moreover, how could one explain in this way dreams in which the relatives and companions of the sleeper appear, as though *their* doubles had come to meet our own? On awakening the sleeper would have questioned them, and they would have told him that they had had quite different dreams from his at the same time, had visited other places or other persons. As this is surely what must most often have occurred, how could primitive man have made a rule of the exceptional cases in which no such contradictions appeared? That would suppose primitive man to have been by far too credulous. Moreover, it is not clear that he tried to explain the problem of the dream to himself. "We constantly pass by problems that we never state, that we never even suspect. . . . Especially when facts are involved that always recur similarly, custom easily lulls curiosity to sleep and we no longer even think of putting questions to ourselves. . . ." This mental laziness is necessarily at its height in primitive man. "Dreams play very little part in our lives. Only vague impressions of them are retained, impressions that are quickly lost." Why should the savage have made such an effort to find explanations for them? "Of the two existences that he leads alternately, daily and nightly, the former must interest him most." How could he have made the second of these, the dream, the basis of all his waking beliefs? On the contrary, it is probably on account of his waking beliefs that primitive man interpreted certain of his dreams in this fashion—those, namely, in which he believed that he entered into relations with religious beings, benevolent or malevolent genies, souls of the dead, etc. "Such dreams were possible solely when the idea of spirits, of souls, of a country of the dead already existed —that is, when religious evolution was relatively far advanced." So these dreams do not serve to explain religion, since they themselves presuppose it.[1]

How, on the other hand, could death have the faculty of transforming the soul into the category of a sacred being and into spirit? Our souls, as our doubles, are in fact "merely something profane, an ambulatory vital principle." But "death adds nothing essential to this, unless it be a greater freedom of movement." Though the soul finally freed from the body may perhaps be more redoubtable, it is no less profane for that reason. Moreover, primitive man holds that the soul closely participates in the body's life. It ages and weakens simultaneously with the latter. "There are peoples in fact among whom no funerary honors are paid to those who have attained senility; they are even treated as though their souls had likewise become so. It even happens that privileged persons, kings or priests, considered as being the receptacles of some powerful spirit the protection of which the society needs to preserve, are regularly put to death before they have attained old age." In such cases it is therefore supposed that this spirit would suffer from the physical decrepitude of those in whom it resides. Far from strengthening the soul, death in this case would weaken it. At all events, death cannot explain

---

1. A study of the interpretation of dreams in other, more or less "primitive" societies has led us to the same conclusions. See this reference in the Bibliography.

a change in the soul's nature—for there exists a natural difference between the sacred and the profane. It is not enough that the souls of the dead are more redoutable, for the fear felt by the believer for things that he adores "is a fear *sui generis*, consisting of respect rather than of terror, in which the dominating emotion is the very special one inspired in man by *majesty*." Now it is not enough that souls be disembodied for them to acquire this character. The natives of Melanesia, for instance, pay no cult to the souls of all the dead but only to the souls of those who already during life were considered sacred, such as priests, sorcerers, chieftains, etc. . . . As for the souls of others, says Codrington, they are "mere nothings, after as well as before death." Thus it is not death that bestows the sacred character upon certain souls, since they possess it already during life.

Above all, however, if the cult of ancestors is the origin of all other cults, it should occupy the principal place in the religious cult of primitive men. Now, on the contrary, "the ancestral cult develops only in very advanced societies like China, Egypt, the Greek and Latin cities; on the contrary, again, it is not found in the societies of Australia," the simplest we know. To be sure, funerary rites and mourning rites occur among them. But a cult is a ritual system *of periodical recurrence.* "No cult of ancestors occurs except when from time to time sacrifices are offered at their graves, when libations are poured there at more or less frequent dates, when festivals are regularly celebrated in honor of the dead. But Australia maintains no intercourse of this kind with its dead." If certain Australian tribes periodically celebrate rites in honor of fabulous ancestors, it is always in honor of personages who, during their lifetimes, were considered as having possessed superhuman attributes. A cult is rendered to them not because they are simply ancestors but because they have always been regarded as semidivine, even during their lives. The Australian has no interest in the dead except at the moment of their death and during the subsequent days or weeks. From such infrequent rites cannot have developed the permanent and periodical cults that permeate a great part of his existence.

Did primitive men, finally, attribute spirits to natural things—to stars, plants, etc.—because they confused the animate with the inanimate? Such cases are adduced as those in which children treat as a living being a table against which they have bumped, forget that their dolls are nothing but dolls, etc. But these are no real illusions but plays of the imagination. Let us confine ourselves to primitive beliefs. "If the spirits and gods of nature are really composed in the image of the human soul, they should bear the mark of this origin and reproduce the essential features of their models." Now the soul is thought of as an inner principle animating the body, maintaining its life and residing in it. But such is not true of the spirits assigned to the various things in nature. The sun god is not necessarily in the sun, nor the spirit of such and such a stone in the actual stone that is its chief abiding place. According to Codrington, in Melanesia the spirit of the sea, the storm, or the forest is not for them what the soul is for the body. The natives think only that "the spirit frequents the forest or the sea and that it has the power to raise storms and to strike travelers with sickness." The spirit, therefore, is usually outside the object to which it refers.

Besides this, if it is really his soul or his spirit that man has thus projected into things, one might expect him to have conceived the first sacred beings in his semblance. This is not so. Anthropomorphism is not primitive: it appears only in fairly advanced civilizations. In Australia "animals and plants are in the first rank of sacred things. Even among the North American Indians the great cosmic divinities who are beginning to be the object of a cult are very often represented under the likeness of animal species. . . . To find a god entirely constructed of human elements one must go almost as far as to Christianity. . . . Even in Greece and Rome, though the local gods were generally represented with human traits, several mythical personages still bore traces of an animal origin: thus, Dionysus, whom we often encounter in the shape of a bull, or at least with the horns of one; thus, Demeter, represented with a horse's mane; or Pan, or Silenus, or the Fauns, etc." Far from having imposed his own shape upon things, animals, and plants, man believed in the first place that his ancestors were beasts or plants. Accordingly, the cult of nature does not derive from the cult of the soul and of the spirits.

But the chief objection we make to animism is that it derives religion as a whole from the illusions of dreams and sees nothing in them but a vast aberration, a sort of mystical delirium. Now, "it is impossible that such systems of ideas as religions, which have held so great a place in history and to which peoples have at all times had recourse to draw the energy needed by them to support existence, are nothing but tissues of illusion." How could such a deception have perpetuated itself? How could morality and scientific thought, which for so long were associated with religion and still bear its imprint, have been derived from mere delirium? Religion is bound to correspond to some natural reality.

The naturalist school, on the contrary, has sought the origin of religious beliefs in nature and among the earliest ideas of nature formed by men. Man is here supposed to have grasped God in things themselves. According to this, there is nothing more solidly based upon reality than religion, because it has its birth in us from the contemplation of the external world.

When the Vedas—one of the oldest written texts that we possess in an Indo-European language—were discovered and men began to discover them, it was observed that in them the gods are designated by names still in common usage, or which once were so, but that these names are those of the chief natural phenomena. Agni, for instance, the name of a chief Indian divinity, means fire (like the Latin: *ignis*). The Sanscrit word *Dyaus*, related to the Greek Zeus and the Latin Jovis, means the radiant sky. It seems therefore that among these peoples "the bodies and forces of nature were the first objects to which the religious sentiment betook itself." Max Müller, the chief representative of this school, believed that this had been true everywhere.

"At the first glance cast by mankind at the world," Max Müller says, "nothing seemed less natural to them than nature. Nature to them was the big surprise, the great terror; it was a marvel and an everlasting miracle. . . . This vast domain thrown open to the feelings of surprise and fear, this immense unknown opposed to all that is known . . . gave the first impulse to religious thought and language." That is, the sensation of a surpassing infinitude, sprung from the contact with natural forces, is religion's point of departure. But man tried to understand these forces, and, since it is impossible to think without speaking, he gave them names. But the words he then used, traces of which survive in the roots of the Indo-European languages, designate the principal manners of human action: the actions of striking, pushing, rubbing, etc. That is why the chief forces of nature were designated "by those of their manifestations most resembling human actions: the lightning was called '*something* that hollows the ground when it falls or that spreads fire'; the wind, '*something* that groans or blows'; the sun, '*something* that darts gilded arrows through space'; the river, '*something* that runs'; etc." Thence arose a series of metaphors that came gradually to be taken literally. Behind the material world was henceforth imagined an entire fictitious world of spiritual beings created out of nothing. "As mythology gradually endowed each god with a more and more extensive and complex biography, the divine personalities, at first confused with objects, finally became distinguished from them and defined."

Let us assume the highly debatable linguistic hypothesis on which this theory rests. What is difficult to understand is why, if men invented religion to account for natural phenomena, they did not sooner or later recog-

nize their mistake. According to Max Müller, this is due
to a mental disease, a verbal delirium: "To conceive of
the supreme god as guilty of every crime, deceived by
men, embroiled with his own wife, beating his children,
was surely the symptom of an abnormal state or mental
disease, or, better still, of pronounced insanity." But such
a mistake, of no practical value, involving merely practical errors, is untenable. If religion were expected to
explain the universe to us and help us to benefit by natural forces, why, since it was false, was it not seen that it
explained nothing?

But, more than this, can such beliefs seem probable
as natural human reactions to the "marvel" of the world?
"What characterizes the life of nature is a regularity
approaching monotony. Every morning the sun rises at
the horizon, every evening it sets; every month the
moon performs the same cycle; the river flows unin-
terruptedly in its bed; the same seasons bring back the
same sensations periodically. . . . Normally nature's
course is uniform, and uniformity cannot produce strong
emotions." Admiration for the great forces of nature,
even the sentiment of infinitude, are not enough to
inspire us with the thought of sacred things and to
separate them by an abyss from the profane world. Yet
no religion exists without the notion of sacredness. Besides, must one believe that primitive man feels himself

"crushed" by natural forces? Far from believing them to be so superior to his own, "he ascribes to himself a control over things that is not his," though the illusion "prevents him from feeling dominated by them." Finally, the great cosmic forces—the sun, the moon, the mountains, the sea, etc.—were not regarded as divinities until a late period. "The first beings to which cults were established . . . are humble vegetables or animals with which man feels himself at least on a footing of equality: the duck, the hare, the kangaroo, the emu, the lizard, the caterpillar, the frog, etc."

In conclusion, as little as animism can naturalism explain the birth of religion. Neither the illusions of a dream, nor the experience of death, nor the sight of nature and the strange imaginings excited by it among earliest mankind can have produced the notion of what is sacred, essential to religion. True, dreams, death, and nature occasion religious beliefs among primitive peoples, but religious thought has probably been applied to such facts and objects as it has to many others; it has probably borne them along in its tide, but its source must be sought for elsewhere.

TOTEMIC FAITHS
IN AUSTRALIA

ETHODICAL RESEARCH PURSUED DURING
the last fifty years by ethnographers
in America and Australia, especially
by MacLennan, Frazer, Spencer, and Gillen and Strehlow, has focused attention on and made more and more
definite the characteristics of a cult and, simultaneously,
those of a whole very primitive social organization that
has been named "totemism." Traces and remains of it

are found in many localities, but among the redskins of America and the aborigines of Central Australia it appears in its clearest form and preserves most vitality. However, while American totemism is already quite advanced and seems almost past, in Australia it seems closer to its origin. Australian societies are indeed the simplest (in a sense, the most primitive) that we can discover. Not only is their technology very rudimentary —the house, even the hut, is still unknown—but their organization on the clan basis is the most rudimentary conceivable. Here we have the beginnings of social life and, it would seem, of religion as well.

Certain authors, to be sure, have maintained that, however crude Australian civilization may appear to us, it nevertheless is not the simplest conceivable but that clans are found elsewhere that have even more clearly preserved the characteristics of really primitive societies. Father W. Schmidt, the most learned exponent of this hypothesis, contrasts with the Australians in this respect the Pygmies—the very small, almost dwarflike, populations found scattered among the Philippines, in certain islands of Indonesia, in Malacca, in the Andamans, possibly in Ceylon, and in the tropical forests of West African Guinea. These clans are supposed to be characterized by "an almost total absence of any stable, definite organization. There is no established authority. Each adult lives with his wife and children, and there exists between these small family groups no permanent bond but merely temporary approaches due to circumstances." Thus, according to Father Schmidt, should we conceive of primitive humanity. Now, among these hordes, in these species of human herds, instead of the totemic faith disseminated among the Australians, we find vestiges of a very pure religion and morality: these people are supposed to possess the idea of a single god, of creation, of a soul distinct from the body, etc. Since they are truly primitive, we should have to admit that the other societies, which must originally have resembled them, have gradually lost the memory of this (doubtless revealed) religion and morality. Far from being primitive, the Australian tribes would then represent simply degenerate, morally or intellectually impoverished, tribes. It would be quite unmethodical, therefore, to seek the origin of religion among them.

To this we may reply first that—while we have abundant and precise observations of the highest order concerning the aborigines of Australia, observations that confirm one another, though made by different authors— on the contrary, we know very little of the pygmies. As M. Mauss has said,[1] "we have nothing but rather poor documentary evidence concerning them. Only the

---

1. *Année Sociologique.* Vol. XII, p. 69.

Andamanians form an exception to this, and . . . Brown and Man (who have studied them most carefully) give an idea of them very different from what Father Schmidt would like to suggest. Of the others we know little. They are poor, decimated tribes, thrust back into forest or desert, whose dialects are related to those spoken by the most advanced societies surrounding them. In all this there is nothing to permit the reconstruction of humanity's initial phase."

Furthermore, as Durkheim has observed,[2] while the Australians represent the simplest type of society, "hordes of this nature have none of the distinctive qualities of human societies. What characterizes these is the existence of a *civilization;* now, how could a civilization be possible in so unstable a mob of individuals, without agreements, without community of effort, with no organization to permit the accumulation of results attained by each generation . . . ? As man is man only in so far as he lives in society—that is, so far as he shares in a civilization, no matter whether crude or of a high quality —it may be asked whether beings composing these supposed hordes were truly human." In conclusion, while apologetics is one thing, the science of religions is another. If one is convinced that God created man and at the same time revealed to him true religion, it will

---

2. *Année Sociologique.* Vol. XII, pp. 52-53.

always be possible to consider as societies that have lost their faith in such savage tribes as those among which no trace of such revelation is found, but no argument based on fact is advanced to prove that they had ever possessed it.

Two basic traits characterize the totemic clan in Australia. ". . . first, the individuals composing it consider themselves bound by a tie of relationship, but by one of a very special nature. This relationship does not mean that they maintain relations of consanguinity with one another: they are related solely through the fact that they have the same name." This identity of name suffices to make them recognize duties toward one another identical with those always imposed upon relatives: "duties of assistance, of feud vengeance, of mourning, of the obligation not to intermarry, etc." On the other hand, what distinguishes the clan from the Roman *gens* or the Greek *genos* (members of which also bear the same name), "is that the name the clan bears is also the name of a definite species of material things, with which it believes that it sustains very special relations," and, notably, relations of kinship. These material things or totems are most often vegetables and animals, much more rarely inanimate objects.

How is the totemic name acquired? In most tribes by birth: the child has the mother's totem for his own. "In this case, as if by virtue of the rule of exogamy (which forbids intermarriage between members of the same clan), the mother is obligatorily of a totem different from that of her husband, and since, on the other hand, she lives in the same place as he, the members of a single totem are necessarily scattered about in different locations according to the chances of the marriages contracted. The result is that the totemic group has no territorial foundation." In other cases the child has the same totem as the father. Since the child lives with the father, the local group includes primarily people belonging to the same totem, except for those married women who possess foreign totems. In such places each locality may be said to have its totem. Finally, in yet other cases the totem is that of neither the father nor the mother: it is that of the mythical ancestor who is supposed to have come to mystically render the mother pregnant at the moment of conception. "A definite technique makes it possible to recognize who this ancestor is and the group to which he belongs."

Phratries, or groups of clans, are distinguished from clans. There are two in each tribe. "Now, in almost all cases in which the phratry bears a name the meaning of which it has been possible to ascertain, this name is that of an animal." There would therefore be totems of phratries. Indeed, the phratry seems to be only a former clan that has been divided: "the present clans would then be the product of this division, and the solidarity that unites them, a memory of their original unity." This occurs especially in North America, where the totemic organization that has existed there for a much longer time than in Australia is also more stable. This is why the archaic phratry system has been able to maintain itself more clearly and in a more sharply defined state. In America "the moral distance between the clans is slight compared to that which separates phratries. The name borne by each of them . . . is a totem in the full force of the term."

"The totem is not merely a name; it is an emblem, a genuine blazon, the analogies of which with heraldic blazons have often been observed. It is an escutcheon, mark, or design that everyone bears in token of the family to which he or she belongs. Among the North American Indians who have developed the techniques of design, of engraving, and of sculpture, totems are painted on shields or on pieces of bark fixed to the end of a rod and serving as ensigns. The totem is painted on the tent or, when the society has become fixed as to abode, on the house wall, and sometimes on posts set up beside the entrance door, on boats, on utensils, and on funerary monuments. In Australia these totemic representations are less common. However, examples are found: sometimes a figure representing the totem is traced on the ground beside the place where the bones of the dead are interred, or "the body is placed in a piece of hollow wood similarly decorated with designs characteristic of the totem." On shields, utensils, and rocks certain of the Australians draw figures of this sort. Most frequently they appear on the human body. Natives reproduce their blazon not only on objects among their possessions, but on their persons: "it is imprinted in their flesh, forms part of themselves, and this sort of representation is much the most important." In general "the members of each clan try to give themselves the exterior appearance of their totem. . . . At certain religious festivals the person assigned to direct the ceremony wears a garment that wholly or partially represents the body of the animal the name of which the clan bears." When the totem is a bird, masks or plumes serve the same purpose. Each clan has a coiffure of its own: "In the clan of the turtle, for instance, the hair is shaved except for six locks, two on each side of the head, one in front and one behind, so as to imitate the paws, head, and tail of the animal." Probably some systems of tattooing and certain mutilations to which natives are subjected tend to give them the appearance of the totem. For instance, in the rain and water clan among the Arunta two upper teeth of a young man are drawn at the time of puberty: according to tradition, this is an attempt "to make the face similar to certain black clouds with light borders, supposed to presage the advent of rain." In any case, at times of religious ceremony those who officiate, and even the spectators, bear totemic designs on their bodies. "One of the principal rites of initiation, the rite that inducts a young man into the tribe's religious life, consists precisely in painting the totemic symbol on his body."

One may therefore expect that the totem is not merely a name but a religious emblem as well. In fact, "it is the very model of sacred things." From this point of view it is interesting to examine the instruments used by the Australians in their rites: The *churinga* are "pieces of polished stone or of wood, of very varied shape but generally oval or elongated. Each totemic group possesses a more or less important collection of them. Now on each of them a design is cut representing the totem of this same group." These *churinga* "are considered to be among the most sacred of objects. No other exceeds them in religious dignity. . . . And so the profane—that is, women and young people not yet initiated"—may not touch, may not even see them, except on those rare occasions when they are allowed to look at them from a distance. They are piously stored in little vaults, consecrated places, the entrances to which are carefully concealed: "women and noninitiates may not approach

them." The same is true of the vicinity. A man pursued
by another who takes refuge in one of them is in sanc-
tuary. Quarrels are forbidden there. They are places
of asylum.

Each *churinga* has all sorts of wonderful properties.
It cures wounds and sickness. "It confers important
powers on the totemic kin and insures its normal reproduction. It gives strength, courage, and perseverance
and, on the other hand, depresses and weakens enemies."
The clan's fate depends on these objects. It is threatened
by the greatest misfortune if they are lost. When they
are loaned to a foreign group, "there is a real public
mourning." Individuals can "use them only with the con-
sent and under the direction of the chief. They form a
collective treasure, the holy ark of the clan." Now the
churinga are objects that are like others except that they
bear "engraved or drawn" upon them the totemic mark.
It is this mark, therefore, and it alone, that confers the
sacred character upon them.

"The *nurtunga* . . . is basically constructed of a vertical support consisting either of a spear, or of several
spears grouped in a sheaf, or of a mere pole. Tufts of
grass are suspended all around the support by belts or
bands of hair. Above these is added down, placed either
in circles or in parallel lines running from top to bottom
of the support. The summit is crowned with plumes of

the falcon eagle." The *waninga* is a vertical support crossed by one or two transverse pieces, which give it the appearance of a cross. Strands of human hair or fur, stretched between the arms of the cross and the ends of the support, form a network. The *nutunja* and the *waninga*, "which figure in a number of important rituals, are the objects of a religious respect exactly like that inspired by the *churinga*." But "the vertical lines or rings of down . . . [and] the strands of the *waninga* must assume a shape rigidly determined by tradition that, in the natives' imagination, symbolizes the totem." They are nothing but a picture of the totem, since each of them serves only for the course of a ceremony and is then taken apart.

Thus that which is sacred is the totemic emblem, "on whatever object it may be represented." Moreover, it may be observed that among the Australians these decorations, highly simplified geometrical designs, have only a very distant likeness to the objects they are supposed to represent. "Only the clan members can tell the sense attached to this or that system of lines. In general, men or women are represented by semicircles, animals either by complete circles or spirals, the outlines of a man or animal by lines of points, etc." They are symbols, not portraits.

While the totemic representations are sacred, the animals, plants, and other objects they represent also arouse religious feelings among the natives. "The sacred nature of the totemic animal or plant appears in the prohibition against devouring it. Probably because they are sacred things they may share in the composition of certain mystic repasts . . . but ordinarily they may not be employed for commonplace diet. Anyone infringing this prohibition exposes himself to the gravest danger; . . . it is thought that the sacrilege automatically causes death." Though these prohibitions are milder in certain cases, they do not entirely disappear: if it is permissible to eat some part of the plant or animal totem, only a little is consumed at a time: or else it is also forbidden to devour the most sacred portions, such as the eggs or the fat. Old men, persons who have achieved a high degree of religious dignity, may eat the sacred thing, but only because they themselves are sanctified. This is why the myths inform us that ancestral heroes, almost divine persons, were freed from these proscriptions. If the prohibition is again intermitted in cases of necessity, when the native is starving and has nothing else to eat, or when the totem, like that of water, is such that man cannot do without it, one must still submit to certain conditions: not draw the water himself, receive it from the hands of someone else, etc. "To the proscription of eating is often added that of killing or, if the totem is a plant, of plucking," to be sure with many exceptions and qualifications, especially when harmful animals are involved. Finally, a few but rather rare cases are mentioned in which man is forbidden to touch the animal or plant totem.

These prohibitions are, finally, fewer and much less strict than those of which the totemic emblem is the object. Totemic animals and plants, unlike the *churinga*, the *nurtunga*, and the *waninga*, are normally involved in the life of every day. The images of the totemic being are more sacred than the animals, plants, etc., they represent.

Let us add that men also in this religious system share the religious quality and sacred character to about the same degree as plants and animals. "The cause of this personal sanctity is that the man believes himself not only a man in the usual sense of the term, but an animal or plant of the totemic variety." The man bears the name of the animal or plant. Now, for primitive man identity of name suggests identity of nature. For in his eyes the name is more than an appellation: it is a portion of his being, to such an extent that those who know it already have a degree of power over the being that bears it. "Therefore each individual has a double nature: two beings, a man and an animal, coexist in him."

To account for this duality of nature, natives have

imagined various myths, inspired by the idea of man's descent from the totemic animal and have imagined that thus there is a relation of kinship between them. Some think that "among the first of men, certain ones had the power of transforming themselves into beasts. Others . . . assign to the beginnings of humanity . . . either inert beings, intermediary between the two kingdoms, or formless creatures, scarcely conceivable, with no sort of definite organ or member. . . . Mythical powers, sometimes thought of in the shapes of animals . . . are supposed to have transformed these ambiguous beings into men. . . . By blows of the ax or (if the operator is a bird) by blows of the beak, the human animal is supposedly sculptured from this amorphous mass, its members separated, its nostrils pierced." Elsewhere it is supposed that the ancestor was a human being, "but one who, through a long course of different vicissitudes, has been led to live for a greater or lesser time in the midst of fabulous animals belonging to the same species as that which has given the clan its name. "He is assumed to have grown so similar to these animals that on his return to the company of men they, not recognizing him, gave him the name of the animal he resembled. Behind all these explanations, different as they may be, one feels the need of a logical explanation for a belief leading to a contradiction in terms—namely, the belief that a man may be at once man and animal.

Thus, in the same sense as plants or animals men are sacred (and there are even certain parts of their bodies, certain tissues, that inspire an especial veneration—for instance, the blood), it serves to consecrate the instruments of the cult. The blood shed by adults and young men in the course of ceremonies of initiation must not be seen by women. The same is true of the hair, of the hair on the sides of the face, of the foreskin, of the fat of the liver. Since man is sacred, he is in no inferior position with respect to the animals or plants the names of which he bears. Totemism is not referable to the cult of animals or of plants, to a sort of "zoolatry" or cult of life. Man does not adore the animal as the believer adores his God: "in a word, the bonds between him and them are much more like those which unite the members of one family." In them he beholds associates whom he summons to his assistance, who guide him on the chase, who put him upon his guard before threatening dangers. In return, he treats them with deference, "but the services he renders them do not in the least resemble a cult."

Up to this point we have distinguished three categories of sacred things: the totemic emblem, the plant or animal; the form it represents; and, finally, the clan members. But we must go further than this. A whole group of external things indeed are attached to the clan. "For the Australian everything in the universe is a part of the tribe; they are its constituent elements and, as it were, regular members; so like men that they have a definite place in the framework of the society. . . . By virtue of this principle, when the tribe is divided into phratries, all known beings are distributed among them. . . . Just like the blacks themselves, the sun, the moon, and the stars belong to one or the other phratry. . . . But this classification does not stop here. The men of each phratry are distributed among a certain number of clans; similarly, things destined to each phratry are in their turn distributed among the constituent clans. Such and such a tree, for instance, will be attributed to the Kangaroo clan—to it alone—and, consequently, like all the human members of this clan, will have the Kangaroo as its totem; another tree will be under the jurisdiction of the Serpent clan; the clouds are classified under one totem, the sun under another; etc. Thus all known beings are disposed in a sort of pattern or systematic classification embracing all nature."

It is extremely noteworthy that such natural classifications, the first encountered in history, have the very divisions of society as their framework. "Because men were in groups, they were able to assign things to groups;

for, to classify the latter, they merely assigned them a place in the groups formed by themselves. . . . The unity of these primary logical systems simply reproduces the unity of society itself." The idea of genus and species that underlies our science could only arise because men had before their eyes the picture of the divisions of society.

No less remarkable is it that men, who thus attached everything that exists to some totem or other, have attributed to all as it were a religious character. In the religions of Greece and Rome, as soon as the gods appear, each of them is "put in charge of a special category of natural phenomena—one that of the sea, another that of the atmosphere, yet another that of the harvest or of fruit, etc.—and each of these provinces of nature will be considered as drawing its indwelling life from the god upon whom it depends." Now in the Australian societies totems already play roughly the same role as will later belong to the gods. For some tribes where there are ten clans the whole world is divided into ten parts, each of which is referred to one of the ten totems. These objects draw their reality and life from the totem. They are so many aspects of it. Indeed, rain, thunder, lightning, clouds, hail, and winter are all included in the Crow clan. They are regarded as different sorts of crows. Thus "far from being restricted to one or two categories of beings, the domain of totemic religion extends to the utmost limits of the known universe. Exactly like the Greek religion, it puts divinity everywhere; the famous formula *panta plere theon* (everything is full of gods) is equally suited to be its motto."

Nor does the analogy cease here. The different totemic cults practiced in each clan are not like the same number of distinct religions, indifferent to one another: they are parts of a single whole, elements of one religion. "The men of one clan by no means consider the beliefs of neighboring clans as indifferently, sceptically, or hostilely as a strange religion is usually considered; they themselves participate in these beliefs. The Crow people also are themselves sure that the Serpent people have a mythical serpent as ancestor and owe to this origin certain special virtues and marvelous powers." Often a man may eat of a totem not his own only when he is authorized to do so by the people of that totem. Members of different clans often attend the rites performed by the peoples of a given totem. "There is even a whole cycle of rites that are exhibited obligatorily before the assembled tribe: these are the totemic ceremonies of initiation." Furthermore, the same totem is never repeated twice in the same tribe, and, since everything is distributed among these totems, there must needs be a preliminary agreement among the different clans of the tribe to assign the limits of these domains. Totemic religion accordingly springs from the combination of the various cults practiced by the clans, "just as Greek polytheism consisted of the combination of all the special cults addressed to different divinities."

But totemism is even more complex than it appears. We have just observed that it tends to exceed the clan limits and that in one respect it is a tribal religion. In another it is an individual cult. "In some Australian tribes and the majority of the Indian societies of North America each individual has a personal relationship to a given thing similar to that which each tribe has to its totem. Sometimes this thing is an inanimate being or an artificial object; but very commonly it is an animal." The individual bears the name of this thing: it is like a first name added to the collective name or totem of the clan. "At least among the American tribes this name is duplicated by an emblem belonging to each individual, which in various forms represents the thing designated by this name." There are close affinities between the individual and his totem. "Man shares the nature of the animal; he has its qualities as well as its defects. For instance, someone with the individual blazon of the eagle is supposed to possess the gift of seeing into the future; if he bears the name of the bear, he is said to be liable to be wounded in fighting, because the bear is slow and heavy . . . ; if the animal is despised, the man is the object of the same disdain. In certain cases—for instance, in danger—it is believed that the man can assume the animal's form." If the animal dies, the man's life is threatened. Thus it is a very widespread rule that the animal must not be killed nor its flesh eaten. "In its turn, the animal protects the man and in a sense serves as his patron saint. . . . Similarly, as it is often considered to have marvelous powers, it communicates these to its human associate. The latter thinks himself invulnerable to bullet or arrows. . . . In return, the individual may influence the animal. He gives it orders. A Kurnai who has the shark as his friend and ally thinks that by means of an incantation he can scatter the sharks threatening a boat."

Although the "individual totem" closely resembles the clan totem, it differs from it in important respects. In the first place, the individual does not consider himself as the offspring of his associate, as the clan is the issue of its totem. It is not a relative. Then, "the members of a clan allow the neighboring clans to eat of their animal totem." The individual, on the contrary, not only respects the species to which his personal totem belongs, but he also tries to protect it against strangers. But, most importantly, these two totems are not acquired in the same way. The clan totem is generally obligatorily transmitted from father or mother to son. In Australia the personal totem is acquired more often through the mediation of a third person, a relative or someone possessing special powers, like an old man or a magician, either at birth or at the moment of initiation. "Methods of divination are sometimes employed for this purpose. For instance, . . . the grandmother or other old women take a little bit of the umbilical cord to which the placenta is attached and make it all describe a somewhat violent revolution. Meanwhile, other old women, seated in a circle, successively propose different names. The name is adopted that is pronounced at precisely the moment when the cord breaks."

Furthermore, the individual totem exists in Australia in only a small number of tribes. Many do not know of it. Sometimes it is reserved for magicians, and sometimes only those who want to excel in war or in the chase secure such protection. But, although individual totemism is "freer and more a matter of choice" than clan totemism, it nevertheless possesses a much greater power of resistance than the latter. "Even though no visible trace of collective totemism exists any longer in civilized countries, the idea that a solidarity exists between each individual and a certain animal, plant, or exterior object underlies usages still to be observed in several European countries."

THE EXPLANATION OF
TOTEMIC INSTITUTIONS:
MANA

T HE FAITHS THAT WE HAVE JUST ANALYZED are certainly religious, since they distinguish sacred and profane things. Furthermore, we do not know or even conceive of any more primitive faiths. Indeed, they are inseparable from the social organization underlying the clan. They would not exist without the clan, and without them the clans would not be distinguished from one another. "Now, the organization underlying clans is the simplest of which we know," since at present no societies have been discovered with but a single clan. "Therefore, if we succeed in discovering the origins of totemism, we have chances of simultaneously discovering the causes that made the religious sentiment manifest itself in humanity."

Certain scholars have thought that totemism derived from the cult of ancestors, which was more primitive than itself, as well as from the doctrine of the transmigration of souls. The religious respect inspired by the ancestor was supposed to have been transferred to the animal or plant in which he was reincarnated. "In Java and Sumatra crocodiles are particularly held in honor; in them beneficent protectors are supposed to exist whom it is forbidden to kill; offerings are made to them. Now the cult thus rendered to them springs from the fact that they supposedly incarnate the souls of ancestors." Beliefs of the same sort are observed among the Philippine Malays, among the Bantus and in Melanesia. But all these societies have developed beyond the phase of totemism. They contain families, not clans. "If one wishes to know how totemism originated, neither Java, Sumatra, nor Melanesia should be studied, but Australia. Here there is neither cult of the dead nor doctrine of transmigration." To be sure, ancestors are reincarnated, but in human bodies, never in the bodies of animals. Besides, in order to believe in the doctrine of transmigration, one must admit a certain relation between man and animal. Otherwise, how should a man's soul pass into an animal's body? "The doctrine of transmigration postulates this peculiar affinity but gives no explanation of it." But the belief in this relation between man and animal is one of the basic principles of totemism. Logically, then, totemism must have come first and belief in transmigration, second.

Other authors have explained totemism by the need primitive men must have felt to secure themselves a protection or shelter against dangers of all sort that beset them. According to Frazer, they believed that they could withdraw the soul from the body and place it in security in an animal's body or in a plant. Indeed, practices exist that have no other purpose but this. "At the moment when people want to enter a newly built house a magician withdraws their souls and places them in a bag, subject to restoring them to their possessors when the threshold has been crossed. This is because the moment of entering a new house is exceptionally critical; one risks disturbing and thus offending the spirits that reside in the ground and especially under the threshold, and if no precautions were taken they might make a man pay for his temerity." Such beliefs are supposed to be at the basis of totemism. But how could primitive man have believed that his soul was more secure in an animal's body than in his own? Would it not then be exposed to whatever might overtake the animal—for instance, to the blows of hunters? This would be attributing too absurd a reasoning to savages.

Furthermore, there arises a preliminary question. Since there are two sorts of totems, the collective and the individual, one must know which preceded the other. If the individual totem was first, one may contend that certain individuals, having tested the efficacy of their totem, have been imitated by others and by the clan. But if the collective totem came first, this is doubtless explained by social conditions or by the very organization of tribes.

Now, a man having an individual totem tries to make his companions respect the animals of the same species as his totem, in order that his protector may not disappear. If the collective totem were derived from the individual totem, the members of the clan would have not only to abstain from eating and killing their totem but would have to require that foreigners also should abstain. On the contrary, every clan by means of certain rites "sees to it that the plant or animal whose name it bears shall grow and prosper in order to secure abundant nourishment for the other clans." Otherwise, it would be incomprehensible also, under this hypothesis, that two clans of the same tribe should always have different totems—as is the case. Why should they not have chosen their totem from the same species?

But, above all, this hypothesis is contradicted by facts. "If individual totemism were the initial fact, it should be all the more developed and all the more apparent the more primitive the societies themselves are. Whereas the opposite is the truth. The Australian tribes are far more backward than those of North America; nevertheless, Australia is the home par excellence of collective totemism. In the great majority of tribes it reigns alone, while there is not one in which only individual totemism is practiced."

Besides, "individual totemism, so far from having given rise to clan totemism, presupposes the latter. It is born and has its being in the framework of collective totemism. . . . Indeed, among the very societies where it preponderates (in America) novices do not possess the right to take any animal at all for their personal totem; but a certain number of definite species is assigned to each clan, outside of which no choice may be made. . . . There even exist cases where . . . the individual totem represents a portion or a special aspect of the collective totem. . . . Each clan member considers the personal totems of his companions as to some extent his own." "Thus the first form of individual religion encountered in history appears, not as the active principle of public religion, but, on the contrary, as a mere aspect of it. The cult organized for himself by the individual, in a sense within his own conscience, far from being the germ of the collective cult, is only the collective cult applied to the personal needs of the individual."

We must accordingly first explain clan totemism. May a common principle be discovered from which derive all the beliefs grouped under this name and which constitutes their unity? "We have seen that among the first ranks of the things held sacred by totemism are the elaborately devised representations of the totem (the emblems); next come the animals or vegetables the name of which the clan bears and, finally, the clan members. Since all these things are sacred by the same right, though unequally so, their religious character cannot depend on any of the special qualities distinguishing them from one another." They are not respected or feared because a totemic emblem is composed of a certain venerated material, nor because a clan member is a man. It is not because an animal or plant possesses certain special characteristics. Something must exist common to all these objects and beings, "a force discoverable in each of them that is nevertheless not confused with any one of them," a force that precedes and survives them and that inspires the religious sentiment whenever it is manifested—an anonymous and impersonal force, conceived now under the animal, now under the vegetable species, now under that of a clan member. "Here is what the emblem really consists in: it is merely the material form beneath which imaginations conceive this immaterial substance or diffused energy permeating all sorts of different beings and which, itself alone, is the object of a real cult." A force at once material and moral, just as "for the Christian, God the Father is the protector of the physical universe as well as the governor and judge of human conduct."

The reason why such an idea does not surpass the mind of primitive peoples is that "either in the anterior societies from which the Australian tribes sprang or in the latter themselves" very similar "conceptions are discovered under an explicit form." "The various totemic principles addressed by the different clans of a single tribe are distinct from one another." But they all play fundamentally the same part. "Now there are societies that have had the feeling of this community of nature and that have consequently raised to the idea of a sole religious power all the other sacred principles of which are only modes and which is itself the unity of the universe. And since these societies are still completely imbued with totemism, since they are still parts of a social organization identical with that of the Australian peoples, we may say that totemism was the mother of this idea."

Similarly, a great many American tribes, especially those of the great family of Sioux, believe that above the separate gods there exists a superior power, which they call *wakan*. It is not a sort of sovereign god. It is not imagined to be a personal being. It has never been seen, and no words can give any idea of it. "All the beings revered by the Dakotas—earth, the four winds, the sun, the moon, the stars—are manifestations of this mysterious life and of this power that circulates through everything . . . the principle of every living thing, every acting thing, every moving thing." Among the Iroquois the *orenda* is the exact equivalent of the *wakan* of the Sioux. "It is a mysterious power," says Hewitt, "conceived by the savage as inherent in all bodies which compose the environment in which he lives . . . the rocks, the water-courses, plants and trees, animals and man, the winds and tempests, clouds, thunder, lightnings, etc." It is the cause of all phenomena, all activities. "A sorcerer, a shaman, participates in the *orenda,* but so does a man who succeeds in all his undertakings." The *manitou* of the Algonquins has no other meaning.

"It is, however, in Melanesia that it [this idea] has

been studied for the first time. True, in certain Melanesian islands the social organization no longer actually has a totemic foundation; but totemism is still perceptible in everything. . . . Now among these peoples there is found under the name of *mana* a notion, the exact equivalent of the *wakan* of the Sioux and the *orenda* of the Iroquois. According to Codrington, it is "a force absolutely distinct from all material force, acting in all sorts of ways, good or evil, which is for man's greatest advantage to submit to his control and to dominate. . . . It is . . . an influence of an immaterial and, in a sense, of a supernatural character; but it reveals itself through physical force, or else through every sort of power and superiority possessed by man. Mana is not fixed to a definite object; it may be directed to every kind of thing. . . . The entire religion of the Melanesian amounts to securing mana for himself, either to profit by it personally or to make someone else do so."

It is indeed true that, at least in the totemic cult, there is not to be found in Australia the idea of a single, universal force, such as mana. This is because in Australia the clan's totemism more than elsewhere reposes on a foundation of organized cult. Although the totemic group is in a sense merely a chapel in the tribal Church, it is an independent one. "The clan totem is completely sacred only for the clan . . . for the group of things appertaining to each clan . . . to the same individuality and to the same autonomy. Each of these is conceived of as being nonreducible to the other, similar groups." Accordingly, it would be impossible to consider these distinct worlds as so many manifestations of one and the same force: on the contrary, one would have to attribute a distinct principle to the things and members of each clan, the action of which would extend no further. "It is with the sense of tribal unity that the sense of the essential unity of the world was awakened." Now Australian totemism is still pre-eminently a clan religion.

In Australia itself magic beliefs are unlike this. "Magic is a tribal, even an intertribal institution. Magic forces do not appertain specifically to any definite part of the tribe." Anyone may influence them if only he possesses sufficient formulas, and everyone is liable to suffer their effects. "They are vague forces radiating over the whole tribe and even beyond it." It is noteworthy that among the Arunda and the Loritja they are conceived of as mere aspects and special forms of one single force called in Arunta *Arungquiltha* or *Arunkulta*. "According to Spencer and Gillen, it is a term of rather vague meaning; but at its source one always finds the idea of a supernatural, evil power. . . . The word is indifferently applied either to the evil influence emanating from an object or to the object itself where it has its temporary or permanent abode." And Strehlow says, for his part, "By *arunkulta* the native means a force that abruptly interrupts life and brings about the death of whoever is instilled with it." This name is given to bones of the dead or pieces of wood from which malevolent charms and animal or vegetable poisons detach themselves. Thus it is quite precisely a noxious mana. "So, since magic forces are conceived of as being all of the same sort, the same would be true of religious forces if Australian totemism were not closely confined and, as it were, multiplied within the framework of the clans." In any case, there is no difference of nature between the magic and religious forces, and, though the latter do not extend beyond the clan's limits, they are nonetheless, like the former, impersonal and anonymous, general and diffused. "The totemic cult is addressed neither to specific animals or plants, nor even to a vegetable or animal species, but to a sort of vague power dispersed throughout things."

Such is the primal conception from which all the ideas and figures of the religions of all periods are derived; it was needed only to imagine that this substance became fixed at a point in space or temporarily assumed this or that form; thence sprang the spirits, demons, genii, gods of every degree. "A Dakota Indian, questioned by Miss Fletcher, expressed in vivid language this essential con-substantiality of everything sacred: everything that moves at one moment or another stops here or there. The flying bird stops at a place to build his nest, at another to rest from his flight. The walking man stops where he pleases. So with divinity (that is, with the power in question). The sun, no matter how brilliant and magnificent, is one place of its alighting. Trees and animals are others. The Indian thinks of these places and directs his prayers thither that they may attain the spot where the god (or power) has taken its station and in order that the god (or power) may obtain assistance for him." Thus, insofar as they share in this power, sun, moon, animals, and likewise the souls of the dead are the objects of rites. At the source of religious thought appear not definite objects and beings but anonymous forces. Particular sacred things are only its individualized forms, and, moreover, there is "no divine personality that does not retain something impersonal."

THE TOTEM AS A
SYMBOL OF THE CLAN:
The Divine Principle Merely Society
Assumed as a Reality

BUT WHENCE ARISES THE IDEA OF THIS diffused, impersonal force that lies at the base of religion? Whence have savages derived it? Where does this force itself exist and of what does it consist? This is indeed the main problem, one to which we now see but a single solution. It is wholly improbable that this religious force is referable to specific qualities that distinguish men and animals or plants from other objects. Why should man, as man, be regarded as a sacred being? Reduced to himself, to his physical qualities, man is little. Reduced to his own strength alone, the individual is more conscious of his own weakness than of anything else. As for sacred animals or plants, those that become totems, they are lizards, caterpillars, rats, plum trees, cockatoos, etc.; no possible reason can be seen why man should have distinguished them from profane objects if he merely adhered to the impressions received from them in the course of daily life. But "we know that the center of the cult lies elsewhere. It is the figurative representation of these plants or animals, the totemic emblems and symbols of all sorts, that have the most sanctity. In them therefore abides the wellspring of religiosity, only a reflection of which the real objects represented by these emblems receive."

In fact, these emblems express two sorts of things. On the one hand, they are "the external, perceptible forms of the totem. But, on the other hand, each "is also the symbol of this definite society called the clan. It is its flag: it is the sign by which each clan is distinguished from the others, the visible mark of its personality—a mark, furthermore, carried by whatever in any sense forms a part of the clan—men, animals, and things. If then it is simultaneously the symbol of God (or the totemic principle) and of society, is not this because God and society are basically one? . . . The clan god, the totemic principle, can therefore be nothing but the clan itself, but the clan conceived of as a reality and represented to the imagination under the perceptible natures of the vegetable or animal which serves as its totem."

In fact, a society "has everything necessary to arouse in men's minds . . . the sensation of divinity; for to its members it is what a god is to those who believe in him." What, indeed, is God? First, a being upon whom man depends and who obliges him to behave in a certain way. "Now, society, too, maintains in us the sensation of perpetual dependency. . . . It compels us to submit to all sorts of restraints, privations, and sacrifices without which social life would be impossible." A god also is a being whom we respect not only because he is more powerful than we, but because we ascribe to him a very strong moral ascendency. Now, for the same reason, society in our eyes has a prestige that dictates to us the same sentiments of respect. At the same time, a god is "a force upon which our strength is founded. The man who has obeyed God and who for this reason thinks that he has him on his side faces the world confidently and with the feeling of increased energy." But society, too, enhances our strength by all that we derive from it and raises us above ourselves. And this not merely under special circumstances; "there is, so to speak, not a moment of life when some afflux of energy does not reach us from without." Since we need the affection, sympathy, and esteem of our fellows, we owe to society all the advantages of civilization. Even though we should not perceive "whence we possess them, we at least know that they are not our own doing." Thus, through the mere fact that we are members of a society, we have a conception of forces that dominate and at the same time support us—"that is, in brief, of religious forces."

It is easy to show how and when the Australian aborigine feels himself simultaneously dominated and exalted by the clan of which he is part, so much so that it seems as though mysterious superior forces were enveloping and transporting him. "The life of Australian societies is divided between two different phases. Sometimes the population is scattered about in little groups pursuing their occupations independently of one another; each family then lives by itself—hunting, fishing, and, in brief, seeking to secure the food indispensable to it by every means in its possession. At times, on the contrary, the population concentrates and condenses for a period varying from several days to several months . . . when a clan or a part of the tribe is assembled in collective

gatherings and when on such occasions a religious ceremony is performed." Now there is a great difference
between these two periods. In the former men are dispersed and lead a "uniform, dull, colorless existence."
In the second, on the other hand, from the mere fact
that they are united, feelings of unusual intensity arise
in them, for the feelings of some echo those of others.
In these ceremonies there are nothing but violent gestures, cries, and shouts, with which blends the strange,
wild music of instruments. A lively excitement reigns.
Passions are unleashed. The entire physical and mental
being is stimulated to the highest degree. In such an
exalted state man no longer knows himself. He feels
"dominated and carried away by a sort of external
power that changes his feelings and acts from their usual
course. . . . He seems to have become a new creature."
So, to judge by their cries, gestures, and attitude, his
companions also feel. "How could such experiences,
especially when repeated daily for weeks, fail to leave
him convinced that there really are two different, wholly
incomparable worlds? One is that in which he dully
drags out his daily existence. On the contrary, he cannot enter the other without also coming in contact with
extraordinary powers that galvanize him to the pitch
of frenzy. The former is the profane world, the second
the world of things sacred."

But if his clan is the true god who is revealed during these religious assemblies in which social life is concentrated and collective thoughts and feelings are intensified, why does the savage not adore the clan? And why, especially, does he represent it to himself in the shape of an animal or plant, and why is it to these images and not to the clan itself that he performs a cult? "The clan is too complex a reality for such rudimentary intellects to be able to imagine it clearly. . . . The aborigine does not even perceive that these," exceptionally powerful, "impressions reach him from the collectivity. All that he feels is that he is lifted above himself and that he lives a different life from the one he ordinarily leads." If now one seeks to know why he associates such impressions with an animal or plant, we reply: Because this animal or plant has given its name to the clan and serves as its emblem. If, furthermore, the clan has thus chosen an emblem, this is because, like any kind of group, it needed a rallying point. Every collective feeling requires to be embodied in persons, formulas, or material objects. These symbols do not serve as mere labels but help bring men together: "by uttering one and the same cry, pronouncing the same word, performing an identical gesture" in the presence of or apropos of a single object, "they become and feel themselves to be in unison with one another." The clan especially could not do without its emblem, for scarcely any society "lacks so much coherence. The clan cannot be defined by its leader, for, if there is not a total lack of central authority, at least this authority is uncertain and unstable. Nor can it be defined by the territory it occupies, for, since the population is nomadic, it is not closely associated with a definite locality. Moreover, because of the law of exogamy, husband and wife are obliged to be of different totems. . . . For all these reasons, representatives of all sorts of different clans are to be found within the same family and yet more so within the same locality. Group unity therefore is perceptible only by virtue of a collective name" and of the emblem about which all clan members rally.

Why have these emblems been taken from the animal and vegetable world? The emblematic figure had to reproduce an object that could be pictorially represented. "On the other hand, these things had to be such as those with which the clansmen were most habitually in relation. Animals more fully satisfied this requirement. For hunting peoples the animal did indeed provide the essential element of the economic environment. . . . Besides, the animal is more intimately associated with the life of man than the plant. . . . The sun, the moon, and the stars, on the other hand, were too distant. . . . Furthermore, before the constellations were distinguished and classified, the starry vault did not provide things sufficiently differentiated to serve as designations for all the clans and subclans of a tribe. However, the variety of flora and especially of fauna were almost inexhaustible." Probably each group adopted as its badge "the most common animal or vegetable near the place where it customarily gathered."

However it may be, since the totem is the emblem and in a sense the banner of the clan, the aborigines naturally refer to this emblem the sentiments evoked in them by the clan itself. A simple object is more accessible to the imagination than a group and its complex action upon us. "The soldier who dies for his standard dies for his country; but actually it is the idea of the flag that is most present to his consciousness." Thus the sign takes the place of the thing. Now, as we have said, the totem is the clan's flag. What does the native see during the course of these religious ceremonies? "On every hand, what offers itself to his perceptions and attracts his attention is the manifold images of the totem. The *waninga*, the *nurtunja* are so many symbols of the sacred being. It is . . . the *churinga* on which are depicted combinations of lines having the same meaning. Or it is the decorations covering the different parts of his own body, which are simply so many totemic marks. How should not this image, recurring everywhere, in all sorts of forms, not assume a rare distinction in all minds? On it are concentrated the feelings experienced," for it is in the center of the stage. "Even when the assembly disperses, it continues to recall and evoke them, for it survives the assembly, engraved on the cult instruments, the rock walls, shields, etc. Through it the emotions experienced are continually maintained and revived. Everything occurs as though at its direct inspiration." Thus it is that the totemic emblem is, as though they were emanations of it, the center of reference of the mysterious forces the seat and true source of which is in the clan. "Since the religious force is merely the collective, anonymous force of the clan and the latter can be represented to men's minds only through the form of the totem, the totemic emblem is like the visible body of the god."

Thus the clan emblem is the sacred object par excellence. And if animals or vegetables of the totemic species are also sacred, though less so, this is because the emblem represents them and claims to be the reproduction of their image. By reason of this resemblance, they ought to inspire a similar respect, and one would think that they embodied the same forces. Because the totemic animal resembles the emblem, it may not be killed and eaten. Men to still a lesser degree share the same character because they are members of the clan of which the totem is the emblem. Both animals and men enter the category of things sacred, the latter because they have the totem as their common emblem and the former because the emblem reproduces their form. Thus men believed that there are bonds of relationship between themselves and the animals; they imagined this relationship subsequently to explain to themselves beliefs and rites the origin and deep reason for which they could not fathom.

From this point of view it is understandable "when the ambiguity arises that envelops religious forces when they appear in history; how they are simultaneously physical and human, moral and material. They are moral powers" for "their authority is only one form of the moral ascendancy exercised by society over its members." But, on the other hand, they are represented by means of material symbols—images of animals, plants, etc.: "they cannot escape being regarded as closely related to material things. They therefore dominate both worlds. They have their abode in men; but at the same time they are vital principles of things. They energize and discipline consciences; but it is they also who make plants grow and animals reproduce their species."

THE SOURCE OF THE IDEAS
OF SOUL, SPIRITS, AND GODS

A S WE HAVE SEEN, THE RELIGION OF
Australian aborigines is not based on
the idea of the soul or on the belief in
spiritual beings, spirits, or gods. Yet this idea and this
belief appear in all religions. If Australian totemism is
really the simplest form of religion and helps us understand what must have been the origin of all religions,
totemism must also be the cause whose effects are belief

in the soul and in the gods. In fact, one can explain how it happens that the latter spring from the former, especially since among natives a rudimentary notion both of the soul and of God is encountered that is still completely involved with totemism's fundamental beliefs.

The Australian forms a very vague, fluctuating conception of the soul as something the form and substance of which are ill defined. It is distinct from the body, since it may leave it during its slumber and at such times escapes from sight. But it is also closely integrated with the organism: it grows and dies with it. It is partly blended with it or with certain of its organs; thence the common rite of devouring human flesh at funerals: "the flesh of the dead is devoured because a sacred principle is supposed to reside in it, nothing less than the soul." When the soul leaves the body at death, it assumes another name and becomes a new being.

How does the savage explain the origin and nature of the soul that he thinks he perceives in himself? According to Spencer and Gillen, "when an individual dies his soul . . . betakes itself to the land of souls; but after a certain length of time it returns to be incarnated anew, and it is these reincarnations which give rise to conceptions and births. These fundamental souls are they which at the very beginning of things animated the ancestors and founders of the clan. At a time beyond which the imagination does not reach [the period of the Alcheringa], beings existed which derived from no other beings. . . . Organized in totemic clans like the men of today, they spent their time in journeys during which they performed all sorts of marvelous actions commemorated by myths. But the moment arrived when this earthly life came to an end. Singly or in groups they plunged into the ground. Their bodies became changed into trees or rocks which may still be seen at the places where they are supposed to have disappeared beneath the earth. But their souls endure perpetually: they are immortal. They even continue to haunt the places where the existence of their first possessors terminated," and which have a sacred character. Now, when one of these souls, wandering about these places, finds its way into a woman's body, "a conception and later a birth are the results." Each individual is thus merely a new form of an ancestor who reappears in a new body. According to Strehlow, not souls but embryos of children, or *ratapa*, detached from a tree or a rock or issuing from a waterhole lying at the place where the Alcheringa's ancestor plunged beneath the earth, are what enter passing women through the hip. In any case, something of the ancestor penetrates the woman's womb and becomes the child.

But these ancestors possessed miraculous virtues: "they

were able to travel upon the earth, beneath it, through the air . . . they made a lake appear where a wall of rock had been or caused a gorge to open and give them passage. . . . They it is who have given the earth its present form. They have created all manner of beings, men, or animals. They are almost gods." Hence the souls of men, either emanations or reincarnations of these ancestors, are themselves also sacred beings. On the other hand, "these ancestors were not men in the strict sense of the word, but animals or vegetables or even mixed beings in which the animal or vegetable element predominated." Souls have the same nature as these ancestors. But is not this fusion of the human and the animal being produced in the totemic principle? Beyond these myths and beliefs, is there not to be found the confused thought that "the soul is only the totemic principle incarnated in each individual?" Indeed, the totem is common to all members of the clan: each of them feels himself in contact with it, as though the totem had penetrated him. "But in thus penetrating into individuals it must inevitably be individualized. . . . Doubtless, in itself, it remains a force foreign and external to man; but the portion each one is supposed to possess cannot but form close affinity with the particular person within whom it resides: it shares his nature; in some degree it becomes his own." Besides, the totem is completely present in each of its parts. "Each has his own portion of it and all possess it completely." In this sense the soul is merely a fragment of the totem.

The close relationship of the soul to the totem is the further result of its often being represented in animal form. In a very large number of Australian tribes, in order to recognize the person guilty of a man's death, "the body is placed on a scaffolding; then, beneath and around the body the earth is carefully flattened so that the least mark becomes easily visible. People return the following day; if an animal has passed that way in the meantime its traces may readily be recognized." Thence is inferred the clan to which the guilty one belongs. So that it is supposed that the murderer's soul has come in the form of the totemic animal. In many other societies the soul is conceived of in the shape of a bird, a snake, a lizard, an insect, etc. "The soul is often supposed to be reincarnated in an animal body. Thence very probably came the widespread doctrine of metempsychosis." But how could the soul do this were it not closely related to the animal?

This explains why the soul has always been considered sacred and contrasted with the body as the religious contrasts with the profane: "if a god is not made of it, at least a spark of divinity is beheld in it."

Moreover, "the character a man thus attributes to himself is not the product purely of illusion; exactly like the notion of the religious force and of divinity, the notion of the soul has its own reality. It is indeed true that we are composed of two distinct parts, opposed to one another like the profane and the sacred, and one may say in a sense that there is a divinity in us. For society, this sole source of whatever is sacred, is not confined to affecting us from without; . . . it is a permanent part of our organism. Within us it excites a world of feelings and ideas that express it but that at the same time are an integral, permanent part of ourselves." All the ideals and ideas evolved by society, more particularly moral ideas, form one entire portion of our being. Though they are within us, we feel that they do not come from ourselves, and through them we have contact with a world that dominates and that surpases us.

"The Australian religions recognize, above the soul, mythical personalities of a superior order: spirits, the hero-bearers of civilization, and even gods properly so called." How have they been led to conceive of such spiritual beings? Let us start from the idea of the soul. A soul is distinguished from a spirit in being attached to a body and practically without influence except upon it. "The spirit, on the contrary, though it is frequently united by intimate bonds with a particular object—a spring, a rock, a tree, a star, etc.—and though it dwells there by preference, may absent itself at will. . . . Thus it has a wider sphere of action. It can affect all individuals who approach it or whom it approaches." After death the soul seems to approximate a spirit. However, a ghost is not a spirit. "It has no definite attributes. It is a stray being upon which no definite task is imposed. . . . A spirit, on the other hand, . . . is set over a certain order of cosmic or social phenomena; it has a more or less precise function to fulfill in the system of the world."

"But there are souls that satisfy this twofold condition and that consequently are spirits in the true sense of the word. Such are the souls of those mythological personalities placed by popular imagination at the beginning of time, the people of the Alcheringa. . . . In one sense they are still souls, since they are considered to have formerly animated bodies. . . . But, even when they led an earthly existence, they already possessed exceptional powers" that they have preserved. "Moreover, they are charged with definite functions." First, they assure the periodic renewal of the clan, being set over the phenomenon of conception. But this is not all. The ancestor also has the task of watching over a newborn child. "Later, when the child has become a man, he accompanies him on the hunt, drives game toward him, warns him through dreams of dangers he may incur, protects him against enemies, etc." He fills the role of tutelary genius exactly like the *genius* of the people of Latium and the *daimon* of the Greeks. "It is believed to haunt ceaselessly the spot where is the tree or rock or perhaps the waterhole that has been formed at the point where the spirit disappeared into the earth upon terminating its first existence." This explains the religious respect inspired by such spots. No one dares to break a branch of this tree—to desecrate these groves and these rocks, in particular—because the ancestor is the spirit of the tree, rocks, etc. "If the spring is supposed to bear relationship to the rain, it will become a spirit of the rain." Thus each ancestor is simultaneously set as guardian over a definite individual and fulfills the function of a sort of *genius loci*.

Above these clan spirits have been superimposed tribal spirits, mythical personalities of a higher order. Indeed, many resemblances exist among ceremonies belonging to different clans. "Since all the clans are only parts of one and the same tribe, the tribe's unity cannot help being felt through all the diversity of the particular cults. . . . The festivals of initiation all include certain fundamental practices—extraction of a tooth, circumcision, subincision, etc.—that do not vary with the varying totems of the entire tribe. . . . Initiation always takes place before the entire tribe or at least before an assembly to which different clans have been summoned. . . . Its object is to introduce the neophyte into the religious life not merely of the clan into which he was born but of the entire tribe. . . . On this occasion occurs the best confirmation of the tribe's moral and religious unity."

To explain the uniformity of these rites, it has been supposed that they had been instituted "by one and the same ancestor who had come to reveal them to the whole tribe." To such hero-bearers of civilization are referred the creation of the *churinga* and their ritualistic use, the practices of circumcision, the institution of prohibition of marriage within certain limits, the discovery of fire, and the invention of the lance, the shield, the boomerang, etc. "These special ancestors could not be assigned to the same rank as the others. On the one hand, the feelings of veneration inspired by them were not restricted to a clan, but common to the entire tribe. Furthermore, all that was most esteemed in the tribal civilization was attributed to them." This is why they were venerated to a special degree and placed above the other ancestor-spirits as heroes or the demigods.

But the Australians have gone yet further and higher along the way of religion. "There are at least a certain number of tribes who have reached the conception, if not of a single deity, at any rate of a supreme deity," a deity occupying a position of pre-eminence with reference to other spirits and genii. Over a very wide geographic area "a considerable number of tribes believe in the existence of a true tribal divinity"—called, usually, Bunjil, Daramulun, or Baiame. "He is immortal, even an eternal being, since he springs from no other. Having for a while inhabited the earth he arose or was carried to heaven and continues to dwell there surrounded by his family. . . . He, as well as they, is often identified with certain definite stars. A power over the others is also attributed to him. He it is who has regulated the course of sun and moon; he gives them commands. It is he who hurls the lightning from the cloud . . . he, whom one addresses when in need of water. He is called the father of men and is said to have created them. According to a legend, Bunjil made the first man in the following way. With clay he formed a statuette; then he danced about it several times and blew into its nostrils, and the statuette became alive and began to walk. . . . At the same time with man, he created the animals and trees; to him are owing all the arts of life, weapons, language, tribal rites. . . . Being the guardian of the tribal morale, he is infuriated when it is offended." He presides above all at initiations, the tribal ceremony par excellence. "Very often he appears there in the shape of an image. . . . The people dance about it and

sing in its honor, and to it true prayers are addressed."
The authority of this supreme god often surpasses tribal
limits. His cult already has something of an international
character.

Besides, there is only a difference of degree between
the great gods and the mythical ancestors. A great god
is a more important ancestor than the rest. On earth
he was a great hunter, a mighty magician, and the
founder of the tribe. Thus faith in the great gods springs
naturally from faith in the ancestral genii: the notion of
the hero-bearers of civilization serves as a medium of
transition. Moreover, "a number of great gods have a
clearly totemic aspect. Daramulun is a falcon-eagle; an
emu was his mother." Similarly, the name of Bunjil
designates a phratry totem. "Baiame, Bunjil, Naralie
seem therefore definitely divinities sprung from phratry
totems," doubtless in the course of initiation ceremonies,
when the tribe awoke to a livelier self-consciousness and
sought to symbolize its unity in a sacred person or figure.
One of the two phratry totems, the basic tribal totems,
was chosen. To explain the exclusion of the other, "it
is supposed that the latter had been defeated in the
course of a conflict with his rival, an idea so much the
more natural as the phratry totems are generally considered as enemies of one another."

Through the idea of the great god, totemism is related to more complex religions. But "this culminating conception continues without interruption the most gross beliefs," which we analyzed in the beginning. "The great tribal god is merely an ancestral spirit who has finally conquered a pre-eminent position. The ancestral spirits" were conceived to explain individual souls. As for these, they themselves were imagined to account for the feeling of each clan member when he experiences in his own way the influence of collective beliefs that arise and develop within the clan. Thus "the unity of the system equals its complexity." We might add that the apparent extravagance and absurdity of these symbols, when taken literally, need not prevent recognition of the profound truth of the faiths they enclose. For beneath all these concepts one single reality is discoverable: the feeling of the unity of the group and all the emotions and confused thoughts attaching to it.

CONCLUSION

RELIGIONS HAVE EXPERIENCED PROFOUND evolutions, and we hesitate to compare the most elaborate religious doctrines of our times with these totemic cults in which, at first, nothing was seen but a gross animal worship. Most certainly there is no question of confusing these modern religions and the practices and beliefs of primitive peoples and of seeing in the latter typical religion. But, simple as they are, it is now no longer doubtful that in them we rediscover, at least in a sketchy state, "all the great ideas and all the chief ritual attitudes that underlie the most advanced religions—the distinction of things into those sacred and those profane and the notions of the soul, of spirit, of mythical personage, and of national and even international divinity"—and also, as Durkheim has demonstrated in the third part of his *The Elementary Forms of the Religious Life*, "a negative cult with ascetic practices in an exaggerated form, rites of oblation and communion, imitative rites, commemorative rites, expiatory rites, [in which] nothing essential is lacking." There is accordingly no scientific reason for opposition to the extension to other religions of the results at which we arrive after the study of this, the religion in question. Immediately upon its appearance religion is what it will forever remain: its form and external aspect will change, but religion will fulfill the same function by identical procedures.

What is this function? If we have studied it in the simplest types of worship and certainly those nearest to their own origin, this is because religion is not there obscured by the whole complicated growth of myths and of philosophical conceptions that will later develop— an additional element, nonreligious in itself, which conceals from us the sight of what is primitive and fundamental. Now we have recognized that religion's chief function was not and could not be to bring men an explanation of the universe. If believers have expected it to do them such a service, how can they have failed to observe that these fantastic imaginings for the most part conflict with the natural order and neither help understand nor foresee it? The center and point of departure of religion is not dogma. "Believers—men who, leading the religious life, know it through daily experience—know well that its true function is not to make us think nor to enrich our knowledge . . . but to make us act and to help us to live. The believer who is in communion with his God is not merely (nor especially) a man who beholds new truths of which the nonbeliever is ignorant; he is a man of greater *power*. In himself he feels more strength, be it to undergo the difficulties of existence or to overcome them. He is, so to speak, raised above the wretchedness of the human lot because he is raised above his own human condition."

Let us not cling, then, to the letter of dogma, dogma that varies from one religion to another. Truly, the savage errs when he attributes to emblems and to animals of certain species a direct power over him or supposes real bonds of relationship between himself and them. But he is not in error when he sets all the members of his clan and the animals and objects with which he associates it, aside and apart from everything else and considers them all as sharing a common life that communicates a sacred character to them. This life is social life, or the richest and highest life to which he is capable of raising himself. The real power exerted by society over them, a power of which they constitute a portion, is incontestable. Savages have often been able to realize their own self-deception, the fact that they were following their imaginations and trying to seek inspiration in them with the aim of forecasting or modifying the order of nature. But religious faith has certainly not been shaken in such tribes. This is because their real concern was for something wholly unlike understanding and explaining nature, but was for their better self-adaptation to their material environment, for the combatting of hunger and disease, and for escaping death. They sought pre-eminently to arouse in themselves feelings of joy and exultation, the blessings of which they had experienced in the gatherings and ceremonies where rites were accomplished. So they continued, discovering that the practice of their worship created in them such exceptionally powerful impressions that they seemed to have changed their own nature and to be transported to another world. What never wavered in them was their confidence, based on so many experiences, in the "strengthening" virtue, creative of power and joy, regardless of the accompanying feeling of dependence, attached to the intense forms of social life. And surely it is the same with every religion. The absurdity of dogma in them is powerless to exert influence, providing that it brings one the comfort of a more exalted, intense inner life.

But does this comfort proceed simply from the community of life? Does the religious life restore the moral power of society? Is God simply the realization of the collective spirit? In our essentially individualistic modern societies the testimony of the consciences of believers would seem to contradict such a theory. The believer refuses to believe that he adores, not such or such a divine personality, but, behind or through its means, a society. What society, in fact? Lay society, religious society, or both? Yesterday's society, that of today, or that of tomorrow?

Shall we put it that the Church claims to be the universal society and that no faith or religion exists without a Church? We shall be answered with the following argument: Religious feelings differ from all those that result only from life in common. Of course, the gatherings and the assemblies for purposes of worship strengthen them. All religions actually presuppose churches. But the Church is constructed around a faith—that is, a totality of beliefs—to the height of which an individual spirit may rise through its own strength. Religious assemblies and societies contribute to the propagation of these beliefs. But they presuppose them. Faith has the greater value the more profoundly its roots are established in all the recesses of the individual soul and the more it is the creation of him who professes it. Is it not true that the religious attitude is increasingly associated for us with the spiritual attitude; that it implies freedom from the things of this world, demands isolation; that the believer wraps himself up in meditation, retires into himself; and that if he does participate in public ceremonies or accept dogmas or observe rites, this is all merely and increasingly for him the framework of the truly religious life, which itself is wholly inner and personal?

Without any doubt religion has become more and more individualized and a matter of the inner life. But first we have shown that in the most obviously collective religions individual worship has its place, that it is a part and something like a necessary consequence of the other. "The religious force that inspires the clan, becoming incarnated in the separate consciousness of individuals, is itself separate. Thus beings of secondary sanctity are created; each individual has his own, conceived in his own image, associated with his most intimate existence, and inseparable from his destiny: such are the soul, the individual totem, the protecting ancestor, etc. Such beings are the objects of a worship that the believer may perform alone, apart from any group; thus this is surely an initial shape of individual worship; . . . of course, of very rudimentary worship. . . . That is, the individual personality is then little stressed. . . . As individuals differentiated themselves to a higher degree and the value of a person became pronounced, the corresponding worship itself assumed more weight in the sum total of the religious life, while it was simultaneously hermetically sealed off from the world without." But, "even though the whole of religion appears to exist in the individual conscience, the living spring from which it is fed still is society." If a greater and greater importance has thus become ascribed to the personality, it is surely because respect for the individual has become something like a social dogma. Without a long, historical evolution, or without a complication and refinement of life due to successive societies, the individual would never have been capable of thus taking his own development—and, as the saying goes, his salvation—as his aim and ideal. There is something so artificial about such an attitude that it cannot have sprung up and maintained itself without the favor, at least the momentarily propitious attitude, of all collective forces. But, precisely like the clan totem, be it plant or animal, among primitive men, or like ancestor worship and the divine figures of other cults, the individual and the personality of us moderns is but a symbol. Collective religious forces are expressed and made definite momentarily in this shape. The cult of the individual is like other cults; that is, it rests on common beliefs. Besides, nothing proves that it is the end of evolution and that other religious societies are not in the future to imagine other symbols.

Furthermore, the sociological theory of religion, far from being derogatory to religion, acknowledges its value and attributes to it a reality long denied it. Since religion fulfills a necessary social function, it is impossible to regard it as an artificial creation and a pure falsehood. Absurd and false as many of its formulas appear to us, it is, in a sense, true with an eternal verity. If to some degree every system of religious beliefs is a fiction, it is a well-founded fiction. Indeed, religion corresponds to unchanging collective needs that develop within every society. "There is something in religion . . . that is destined to outlast all particular symbols within which religious thought has successively enveloped itself. No society can exist without feeling the necessity of maintaining and confirming at regular intervals the collective feelings and ideas that constitute its unity. . . . Now, such moral sustenance is only possible through gatherings in which individuals . . . reaffirm in community their common sentiments. . . . What basic difference is there between a gathering of Christians celebrating the principal dates of Christ's life or of Jews celebrating either the Exodus from Egypt or the promulgation of the Decalogue and an assemblage of citizens commemorating the foundation of a new moral charter or some great event in the life of the nation?"

The gods die when the nations die because "the gods are only the nations conceived symbolically." Gospels are no more eternal than peoples or societies. But "there is, on the other hand, no reason for believing that humanity will henceforward be incapable of conceiving them anew."

Science and religion are sometimes regarded as opposites, and it is widely conceived that each position conquered by science is finally lost to religion, so much so that religion's destiny is comparable to that of those savage tribes that cannot continue to exist in the presence of and in contact with civilization. But if religion is a social function (rather than a sort of malady or aberration of collective thought), then, since all the functions of society are bound up with one another, if there is any antagonism between them, this is true only when one of them trespasses on the sovereignty of the other.

Actually, both have the same origin. The primary sources of superior spiritual functions spring, just as do religious beliefs, from the focus of social life, inflamed periodically in festivals, ritual ceremonies, or gatherings in which the clan and the tribe become intensely aware of their own existence. All of science and all of morality spring from this source. Religion was the matrix when science slowly developed, and the chief scientific and philosophical ideas have long retained and still partially retain the mark of this origin. "The great service done to thought by the religions is to have constructed a first conception" of the world, and of the relations supposed to exist among things. To be sure, this picture was inexact and bears no resemblance to that nowadays presented by science. But the prime essential was less to succeed than to make the effort. "The primary forces with which human intelligence peopled the universe were elaborated by religion"; since then men have reflected upon these primary ideas and slowly transformed them; but without this starting point science would probably never have come into existence. It is easily conceivable that they should subsist side by side today, since the domain of one is action and life, the sovereignty of the other, knowledge.

BIBLIOGRAPHY

1. Works on Religion by Durkheim

"La prohibition de l'inceste," *L'Année sociologique*, Vol. I. Paris: Presses Universitaires de France (Published by F. Alcan), 1896-1897.

"De la définition des phénomènes religieux," *ibid.*, Vol. II, 1897-1898.

"Sur le Totémisme," *ibid.*, Vol. V, 1900-1901.

"Sur l'organisation matrimoniale des sociétés australiennes," *ibid.*, Vol. VIII, 1903-1904.

Les formes élémentaires de la vie religieuse. Le système totémique en Australie. Paris: F. Alcan, 1912. *(The Elementary Forms of the Religious Life.* Glencoe: The Free Press, n. d.)

"Le problème religieux et la dualité de la nature humaine," *Bulletin de la Société française de philosophie*, March, 1913.

2. *Studies in the science of religion published as Monographs or Works of L'Année Sociologique*

Durkheim, Émile and Marcel Mauss. "De quelques formes primitives de classification. Contribution à l'étude des représentations collectives," *L'Année sociologique*, Vol. VI, 1901-1902.

Hertz. "Contribution à une étude sur la représentation collective de la mort," *ibid.*, Vol. X, 1905-1906.

Hubert, Henri Pierre Eugène and Marcel Mauss. "Essai sur la nature et la fonction du sacrifice," *ibid.*, Vol. II, 1897-1898.

———. "Esquisse d'une théorie générale de la magie, *ibid.*, Vol. VII, 1902-1903.

———. *Mélanges d'histoire des religions.* Paris: F. Alcan, 1909.

Lévy-Bruhl, Lucien. *Les fonctions mentales dans les sociétes inférieures.* Paris: F. Alcan, 1910. *(How Natives Think.* Translated by Lilian Clare. New York: A. A. Knopf, 1926.)

———. *La mentalité primitive.* Paris: F. Alcan. 1910.

3. *Other works mentioned in this book*

Burnouf, Eugène. *Introduction à l'histoire du bouddhisme indien,* 1844. 2nd ed. 1876. *[Legends of Indian Buddhism.* Translated with an Introduction by Winifred Stephens. *(Wisdom of the East Series)* London: J. Murray, 1911.]

Codrington, Robert Henry. *The Melanesians.* Oxford, 1891.

Dorsey, James Owen. "Siouan Sociology," in *United States Bureau of American Ethnology. Fifteenth Annual Report, 1893-94.* Washington, 1897.

Frazer, James George. *The Golden Bough* (3rd. ed.). 3 vols. London: Macmillan Co., Ltd., 1910.

———. *Totemism and Exogamy.* 4 vols. London: Macmillan Co., Ltd., 1910.

Fletcher, Alice. "A Study of the Omaha Tribe," in *Smithsonian Report for 1897.*

Halbwachs, Maurice. "L'interprétation du rêve chez les primitifs," *Journal de Psychologie,* July, 1922.

Hewitt. "Orenda and a Definition of Religion," *American Anthropologist,* 1902.

Howitt, Alfred William. *The Native Tribes of South-East Australia.* London: Macmillan Co., Ltd., 1904.

Müller, Friedrich Max. *Introduction to the Science of Religion.* London: Longmans, Green, and Co., 1873.

Oldenberg, Hermann. "The Religion of the Veda," in *Ancient India its Language and Religions.* Translated by O. W. Werzer. Chicago: The Open Court Publishing Company, 1896.

———. *Buddha: His Life, His Doctrine, His Order.* Translated by William Hoey. London: A. L. Humphreys, 1904.

Spencer, Baldwin and F.-J. Gillen. *The Native Tribes of Central Australia.* London, 1899.

———. *The Northern Tribes of Central Australia.* London, 1904.

Spencer, Herbert. *First Principles.* New York: D. Appleton and Co., 1883.

Schmidt, Father Wilhelm. *Die Stellung des Pygmœen Voelker in der Entwickelungsgeschicte des Menschen.* Stuttgart: Strecker and Schroeder, 1910.

Strehlow, Carl. *Die Aranda-und Loritza-Stämme in Zentral-Australien, 7 fascicules.* Frankfurt am Main: (Stadtisches Volkenmuseum. Veroffentlichungen. No. 1) J. Bauer and Co., 1907.

Tylor, Sir Edward Burnett. *Primitive Culture.* 2 vols. London: J. Murray, 1873.